The Love that Remains

Gentle Reflections for Caregivers Loving Through Dementia

Dr. Toyin Olubiyi

Olubiyi Press

Richmond, VA

Published by: Olubiyi Press
Printed in the United States of America

ISBN: 979-8-9944541-0-7

Table of Contents

Dedication

For my mom.

For the love that remains,
even as memory fades.

For every daughter
learning how to love
in the space between
who a parent was
and who they are becoming.

May you find gentleness and grace
for them —
and for yourself.

Acknowledgments

This book exists because love surrounded me, even in a season that often felt isolating.

To my siblings — my sister, her husband and my two brothers — thank you! Though distance and circumstance shaped how each of us could show up, your care, support, and shared love for our mom mattered more than you may ever know. I am grateful we have walked this road together, each in the way we were best able.

To my husband, thank you for carrying this season with me. For your patience, steadiness, and willingness to support not only me, but my mom as well. Your presence made this journey lighter than it otherwise would have been.

To my children — thank you for your flexibility, compassion, and the grace you offered in ways you may not yet fully understand. You learned alongside me what it means to love across generations.

To the family and friends who called, checked in, listened, prayed, showed up, and supported us in more ways than one — thank you. Your kindness, consistency, and quiet care reminded me that we were not alone, even on the hardest days.

And to my daughter and my brother-in-law, thank you for reading these pages so thoughtfully and for the care you put into your edits. Your time, insight, and gentle attention helped shape this book more than you know, and I am deeply grateful for the love you brought to the process.

This book is held by all of you.

Introduction

There is a kind of grief that does not begin with goodbye.

It begins while the person you love is still here —
still breathing,
still present,
yet slowly becoming unfamiliar.

This book was born in that space.

I am a daughter caring for a parent with dementia.
And like many daughters, I did not recognize what was happening at first.

When my mom began forgetting things, we told ourselves it was age.
She could remember some things clearly and struggle with others.
She laughed.
She functioned.
She insisted she was fine.

So we did not take it seriously.

By the time the truth became undeniable, something precious had already begun to slip away.

There were moments I felt I had finally learned how to manage this season —
only to be met with another decline.
Each change asked me to grieve again.

I learned to cherish what she could still do today, knowing it might be gone tomorrow.

One day — whether in this life or the next — she will be made whole again,
in ways no illness can undo.

Until then, love remains.

If you are holding this book, I want you to know this:

You are not doing this wrong.
You are not failing. This hurts.

And you are not alone in the quiet work of loving someone through loss.

This book is an offering.
A place to rest.
A place to be honest.
A place to breathe.

You are welcome here.

A Note on How to Use This Book

This book is not a guide to managing dementia, not a manual, or a source of medical advice.

What you will find instead is companionship.
Language for grief that is ongoing.
Permission for feelings that arrive without warning.

It is a companion — written from lived experience, not expertise.

This is a book for daughters and caregivers who are grieving someone who is still alive.
For those learning how to love without reciprocity.
For those navigating responsibility, devotion, exhaustion, and faith — all at once.

Although this book is written from my experience as a daughter caring for her mother, many of the reflections may resonate with anyone loving a parent, spouse, or family member through dementia.

You will not find instructions or solutions in these pages. What you will find are reflections offered gently, for moments when words are hard to come by.

There is no right way to read this book. You may move through it slowly, skip sections, return to certain chapters, or set it down when you need to. There is no lesson to master and no progress to measure.

This book is intentionally brief. As a caregiver myself, I understand the many demands on your time and heart. These pages are meant to offer gentle companionship in a form that's easy to pick up whenever you need a moment of encouragement.

If these pages help you feel less alone in this season, then they have done what they were meant to do.

Chapter 1
Grieving Someone Who Is Still Alive

No one prepares you for this kind of grief.

I knew dementia would take my mother's memory. I knew it would change her abilities, her independence, her sense of time. What I did not know was that it would ask me to grieve her while she was still here.

This grief does not arrive all at once. It comes quietly, layered into ordinary days. It shows up in moments that seem small but leave a lasting ache.

Grief does not wait for death. It begins when what you love starts to disappear.

There is a particular loneliness in this kind of loss. The person you are grieving is still breathing, still present, still part of your daily life. And yet, something essential has shifted.

You are expected to carry on as though nothing has changed — because, outwardly, everything looks the same. But inwardly, you are adjusting to absence while practicing presence.

Dementia takes in pieces.

A memory here. A sentence there. A familiar response that no longer comes.

And every piece matters.

Each loss asks something of you. Each change requires a quiet recalibration — of expectations, of hope, of what love looks like now.

This kind of grief has no clear rituals. There are no condolences, no funerals, no formal goodbyes. Just an ongoing reckoning with what has been lost — and what is still being lost.

And yet, love remains.

Love stretches. Love adapts. Love learns to stay present in the midst of uncertainty.

If you are grieving someone who is still alive, know this: you are not confused, and you are not alone. What you are experiencing is real.

This is grief — just not the kind most people recognize.

Reflection

What moments have made you realize that you are grieving someone who is still here — and how have you carried that quietly?

A Prayer

God,
Meet me in this unfamiliar grief.

Help me hold love and loss together,
without needing to resolve either.

Give me grace for what I am losing,
and strength for what I am still carrying.

Amen.

Permission for Today

You are allowed to grieve — even while she is still here.

Reflection

Chapter 2
The Day Our Conversations Ended

I assumed the change would be gradual —
that conversation would thin slowly,
that meaning would fade in pieces small enough to
prepare for.

But there was a moment when I knew.

She was speaking, but the thread was gone.
Her words no longer carried thought from beginning to
end.
I could hear her voice, but not her reasoning.

And something in me understood, quietly and clearly:
our conversations — as we had known them — were
ending.

I lost more than words that day.

I lost counsel.
Reassurance.
The ease of being known without explanation.

For much of my life, conversation had been how my mother mothered me.
She listened.
She advised.
She offered perspective when I could not see clearly on my own.

And suddenly, that exchange was no longer available.

Dementia does not only take language.
It takes shared understanding.

There came a point when I realized that loving her meant protecting her from more than decline.

I had to begin shielding her from the world.

Phone calls became especially difficult. People who did not understand what was happening would speak to her as they always had, unaware of how disorienting those conversations had become.

She struggled to find the right words. She would say one thing and mean another. Sometimes she sounded confident even when she was deeply confused.

What others heard as incoherence, I heard as vulnerability.

Once, someone told another person that my mom had a mental illness because she was not coherent on the phone. Hearing that cut deeply — not only because it was inaccurate, but because it stripped her of dignity in a moment when she needed protection most.

I realized then that not everyone needed access to her.

Shielding her was not about hiding her condition. It was about preserving her dignity. It was about limiting exposure to conversations that confused, frightened, or diminished her.

This, too, was grief.

Grief in recognizing that the world would not automatically soften for her. Grief in accepting that I would sometimes need to stand between her and misunderstanding.

Loving her meant becoming her buffer —
not out of control,
but out of care.

I found myself adjusting — finishing her sentences,
filling in gaps, carrying the weight of clarity for both of us.
At first, I thought this was temporary.
That if I slowed down enough, spoke carefully enough,
we would find our way back.

But dementia does not retrace its steps.

There came a point when conversations became one-sided.
Not because she stopped speaking —
but because meaning could no longer be sustained.

I learned to listen differently.

Not for logic,
but for emotion.

Not for coherence,
but for need.

Sometimes she spoke from old memories, as though
they were happening now.
Sometimes she repeated the same thought, unaware it
had already been said.
Sometimes her words sounded certain — but did not
reflect reality.

And I learned not to correct her every time.

Correction often brought frustration, not clarity.
Explanation increased confusion.
What she needed was not accuracy.

She needed gentleness.

Losing conversation was its own kind of grief.

It meant losing the ability to process life together.
To reflect aloud.
To be mirrored and understood in the way only a
mother can offer.

I still long for her voice —
not just the sound of it,
but the wisdom it once carried.

And yet, even here, love adapted.

Conversation was no longer the bridge between us.
But presence remained.

And I began to learn that connection does not disappear
when conversation ends —
it changes its language.

Reflection

What have you lost in the fading of conversation — and
how have you been learning to listen differently?

A Prayer

God,
Meet me in the silence where conversation once lived.

Help me grieve what has been lost
without closing my heart to what still remains.

Teach me to listen beyond words,
and to love without needing to be understood.

Amen.

Permission for Today

You are allowed to grieve the loss of conversation —
even while love remains.

Chapter 3
When My Mother Could No Longer Mother Me

There was no single moment when the roles shifted.

No announcement.
No clear line where I could say, this is when it changed.

Instead, it happened quietly —
in small exchanges that left me unsettled long before I could name why.

Her judgment began to change.

She could remember certain things clearly,
yet struggle with others that once came easily.
She would say one thing and mean another,
and I learned that listening now required
interpretation.

I realized that she could no longer anticipate my needs
—

or even recognize them —

and that something fundamental in our relationship had shifted.

I was no longer being mothered.

And in its place, something else emerged.

I became the one who noticed first — the small shifts before they became losses.
The one who planned ahead.
The one who learned to anticipate what she could not articulate.

Sometimes she did not have the words for what she needed.
Sometimes she asked for one thing when she meant something else entirely.
And slowly, I learned to read beyond language —
to pay attention to tone, restlessness, and repetition.

Her brain would get caught in old memories.
She would worry about things that no longer needed attention.
At times, she followed me from room to room, unsettled, searching.

And I noticed something else.

When her eyes were on me, she felt safe.

It was not logic that reassured her.
It was presence.

If she could see me,
if she knew I was near,
something in her body relaxed.

In those moments, I understood that I had become her
anchor.

This realization was heavy.

I was grieving the loss of being cared for
while learning how to care in a new way.

There were days I longed for her guidance —
for her discernment, her perspective, her ability to see
me clearly.
I missed being able to lean without thinking about who
would hold whom.

And yet, love remained.

It took on a different shape —
one that required attentiveness, patience, and
steadiness.

Mothering, I learned, is not only about providing.
Sometimes it is about receiving.

And daughterhood, in this season,
meant learning how to offer safety
instead of seeking it.

Reflection

In what ways have the roles in your relationship shifted
— and what has that change asked of you?

A Prayer

God,
Hold me in the space between who she was to me
and who I am becoming for her.

Give me grace for what I have lost,
and strength for what I am being asked to carry.

Amen.

Permission for Today

You are allowed to grieve the loss of being mothered —
even as you learn how to mother in return.

Reflections

Chapter 4
Loving Her in Fragments

I had to learn how to love in pieces.

Connection no longer came as a continuous experience
—it arrived in moments.

Brief.
Real.
Fleeting.

A smile that appeared and disappeared.
A sentence that started strong and faded midway
through.
A look of recognition that lingered just long enough to
matter.

At first, these fragments frustrated me.

I wanted continuity.
I wanted wholeness.
I wanted the version of love I had known before.

But dementia does not offer fullness.
It offers presence in fragments.

And I had to decide whether I would reject those
fragments
because they were incomplete —
or receive them because they were still real.

I learned that love does not lose its value
simply because it is brief.

A moment of clarity still carries meaning.
A short exchange can still be sacred.
A shared laugh, even if quickly forgotten, is still shared.

There were days when connection felt impossible.
When she seemed distant, unreachable, closed off.

And then, without warning, a fragment would appear.

A familiar phrase.
A touch that carried memory.
A look that said more than words could.

I learned to stop demanding permanence.

To stop measuring connection by how long it lasted
and start honoring it for showing up at all.

Loving in fragments required me to let go of
expectations —
not love itself.

It taught me to stay present without grasping.
To receive without trying to preserve.
To be grateful without insisting that moments repeat
themselves.

Dementia fractures experience,
but it does not erase relationship.

Love still moves through the cracks.

And when I learned to meet her there,
I discovered that fragments were not failures.

They were invitations.

Reflection

What fragments of connection have you learned to notice — and how have they changed the way you love?

A Prayer

God,
Help me recognize love when it arrives quietly.

Teach me to receive what is given
without longing for what used to be.

Let me be present for the moments that come,
even when they do not stay.

Amen.

Permission for Today

You are allowed to treasure what is brief —
it still counts as love.

Reflections

Chapter 5
The Guilt of Wanting a Break

I did not expect guilt to be one of the heaviest parts of caregiving.

I expected exhaustion.
I expected sadness.
I expected moments of frustration I would later regret.

What I did not expect was how much guilt would accompany the desire to rest.

Wanting a break felt like a betrayal.

If I was tired, I questioned my love.
If I felt overwhelmed, I questioned my capacity.
If I imagined time away, I wondered what it said about my devotion.

I told myself I should be able to do more.
Carry more.
Endure more.

After all, she was the one who was ill.
That was the story guilt told me.

But guilt has a way of distorting truth.

It convinced me that love and limits could not coexist.
That needing rest meant I was failing her.
That asking for relief meant I was abandoning my role.

None of that was true.

Caregiving is not sustained by self-sacrifice alone.
It is sustained by sustainability.

Love that never rests eventually hardens.
Care that never pauses becomes brittle.

I learned — slowly and imperfectly — that wanting a
break did not mean I loved her less.
It meant I was human.

Rest was not an escape from responsibility.
It was a return to myself.

When I allowed myself space — even briefly —
I returned more patient, more grounded, more present.

Guilt had told me that stepping away would cost me
connection.
What it actually restored was capacity.

I began to understand that love is not proven by how
depleted you are.
It is revealed by how faithfully you return.

Taking a break did not diminish my care.
It preserved it.

And learning to release guilt — even a little —
became one of the quiet ways I learned to love her well.

Reflection

What feelings arise when you imagine taking a break —
and where do you notice guilt showing up?

A Prayer

God,
Release me from the guilt that confuses exhaustion with
devotion.

Teach me that rest is not selfish,
but a form of stewardship.

Help me care without hardening,
and love without losing myself.

Amen.

Permission for Today

You are allowed to rest —
without questioning your love.

Reflections

Chapter 6
When Reassurance Replaces Words

There came a point when words no longer worked the way they used to.

Explanations confused her.
Details overwhelmed her.
Logic no longer brought comfort.

What she needed most was reassurance.

She would ask the same questions repeatedly —
sometimes within minutes —
not only because she had forgotten the answer,
but because her sense of safety had slipped.

At first, repetition frustrated me.

I wanted to explain better.
To find the right words.
To help her understand what was happening.

But understanding was no longer the goal.

Reassurance was.

I learned that repetition was not regression.
It was regulation.

Each question was an attempt to steady herself.
Each repeated concern was a request for calm.

So I learned to respond differently.

Not with new information,
but with familiar comfort.

Not with correction,
but with presence.

I learned to say the same things —
gently, patiently, consistently —
even when it felt inefficient or unnecessary.

"You're safe."
"I'm here."
"You're not alone."

These words mattered more than explanations ever could.

Her brain could no longer hold complexity,
but her body still recognized tone.
Her spirit still sensed care.

When reassurance replaced words,
our communication simplified —
but it did not disappear.

I began to understand that love does not always sound wise.
Sometimes it sounds repetitive.

Sometimes it sounds like calm offered again and again,
without irritation,
without urgency.

Reassurance became the language dementia still understood.

And learning to speak it —
without resentment,

without rushing —
became another way I learned to love her well.

Reflection

Where have you noticed reassurance bringing more peace than explanation?

A Prayer

God,
Help me respond with gentleness
when repetition tests my patience.

Teach me to offer reassurance freely,
without needing to be understood.

Let my presence speak
when words no longer can.

Amen.

Permission for Today

You are allowed to repeat reassurance —
it is not wasted effort.

Reflections

Chapter 7
Asking for Help Without Shame

For a long time, I believed I should be able to do this
alone.

Not because anyone told me to —
but because caregiving quietly convinces you that
needing help is a sign of failure.

I told myself that if I loved her enough,
if I organized better,
if I pushed a little harder,
I would be sufficient.

But caregiving has a way of exposing limits —
not as weaknesses,
but as realities.

There came a point when doing everything myself
was no longer sustainable.

I was tired in ways rest did not easily fix.
I was stretched thin emotionally, physically, spiritually.
And still, I hesitated to ask for help.

Asking felt vulnerable.
Exposing.
Like admitting I was not strong enough for the role I
had been given.

But what I eventually learned was this:
asking for help did not diminish my devotion.

It clarified it.

It meant I was choosing care over control.
Longevity over pride.
Faithfulness over appearance.

When I began to let others in — even in small ways —
something shifted.

Not everything became easier.
But it became lighter.

Help did not replace my role.
It supported it.

It allowed me to show up with more patience,
more steadiness,
more capacity to love.

I learned that caregiving was never meant to be solitary.

It is sustained by community —
by shared responsibility,
by honest acknowledgment of need.

Asking for help did not mean I was stepping away.

It meant I was choosing to stay.

Reflection

What makes asking for help difficult for you — and
what kind of support might ease this season?

A Prayer

God,
Release me from the belief that I must carry everything alone.

Give me the humility to ask,
and the grace to receive.

Help me trust that accepting help
does not weaken my love,
but strengthens it.

God, in the moments when I reached my limit, I found You waiting there.

Thank you for the quiet grace that met me in my weakness and reminded me that I was never carrying this alone.

Amen.

Permission for Today

You are allowed to ask for help —
it is an act of wisdom, not failure.

Reflections

Chapter 8
Loving Her While Letting Go

Letting go did not come naturally to me.

For a long time, I believed love meant holding on —
to routines,
to expectations,
to the way things used to be.

I tried to preserve what was familiar.
I resisted change, hoping that consistency might slow
the inevitable.

But dementia does not negotiate.

It requires a different kind of faith —
one that loosens its grip without withdrawing its love.

I learned that letting go was not the opposite of
devotion.
It was devotion, reshaped.

Letting go meant releasing the illusion of control.
Accepting that I could not manage outcomes,
only my presence within them.

It meant grieving what was no longer possible
without closing my heart to what still was.

Some days, letting go looked like simplifying
expectations.
Allowing plans to change.
Adjusting the pace of life to match hers.

Other days, it looked like surrender —
trusting God with what I could not fix,
and releasing myself from the burden of trying.

Loving her while letting go required humility.

It asked me to show up without insisting on
improvement.
To care without attaching my peace to progress.
To remain steady even as circumstances shifted.

I learned that love does not require control to be faithful.

In fact, love often deepens
when it releases the need to manage.

Letting go did not mean loving less.

It meant loving differently —
with open hands,
a softened heart,
and a deeper trust.

Reflection

What are you being asked to release in this season —
and how might letting go make room for peace?

A Prayer

God,
Help me loosen my grip
without hardening my heart.

Teach me to trust You
with what I cannot control,

and to remain present
even when outcomes are uncertain.

Amen.

Permission for Today

You are allowed to let go —
love does not disappear when control is released.

Reflections

Chapter 9

The Loneliness No One Sees

Caregiving is rarely loud.

Most of it happens quietly —
in routines repeated,
in vigilance gone unnoticed,
in responsibility carried without audience.

From the outside, life can look unchanged.
The house still runs.
Conversations continue.
Smiles are offered when expected.

But beneath that normalcy,
there is a loneliness that settles in slowly.

It is the loneliness of holding knowledge others do not
carry.
Of carrying responsibility — even when supported —
that cannot be fully handed off.
Of being the one who notices decline
long before anyone else does.

Even when people are kind,
they cannot fully enter this space.

They visit.
They check in.
They sympathize.

But caregiving is lived, not observed.

There were moments when I felt unseen —
not because people did not care,
but because they could not grasp the weight of
constancy.

I was never fully off-duty.
Even in rest, my attention remained alert.
Even in conversation, part of me was listening for her.

Loneliness, I learned, does not always come from being
alone.

Sometimes it comes from being responsible.

From carrying concern that cannot be set down.
From loving someone whose world is narrowing
while yours must expand to hold it.

And yet, even here, there was grace.

I began to recognize that loneliness did not mean
abandonment.
It meant I was walking a path few could walk with me.

Naming that loneliness —
without resentment,
without self-pity —
was an act of honesty.

And honesty made room for compassion.

For myself.
For others who could not fully understand.
For the quiet strength this role required.

Loneliness did not define this season.

But acknowledging it
kept my heart from hardening.

Reflection

Where have you felt unseen in this season — and what
has helped you stay open?

A Prayer

God,
Meet me in the quiet places where loneliness lingers.

Remind me that even when others cannot see this work,
You do.

Give me strength to remain soft,
and courage to name what is real.

Amen.

Permission for Today

You are allowed to name your loneliness —
it does not diminish your love.

Reflections

Chapter 10
Learning to Love Who She Is Now

One of the hardest lessons of this season
has been learning to love who she is now —
not who she used to be.

I carried memories of her strength, her clarity, her
authority.
I held them close, sometimes too tightly.

Without realizing it, I compared the present to the past-
measuring moments by what was missing
instead of noticing what remained.

That comparison quietly created distance.

I learned that loving her well required a shift —
not in devotion,
but in expectation.

Who she is now is not a lesser version of who she was.
She is different —
and still worthy of full presence and respect.

This meant meeting her where she was,
without trying to pull her back to where she could no
longer stand.

It meant letting go of correction as connection.
Letting go of reminders meant to orient her
but only unsettled her.

Instead, I learned to enter her world.

To respond to what she felt,
even when the facts no longer aligned.

To honor her dignity,
not by insisting on accuracy,
but by preserving peace.

Loving her as she is now
required me to release grief in layers.

Each stage asked something new of me —
a softer gaze,
a quieter presence,
a deeper patience.

I learned that acceptance did not come all at once.

It arrived gradually,
through daily choices
to love without comparison.

And in those moments —
when I stopped wishing she were different
and allowed her to simply be —
love felt lighter.

Not because the season became easier,
but because my resistance softened.

Loving who she is now
has taught me that love is not anchored in memory.

It is anchored in presence.

Reflection

Where might comparison be keeping you from fully
loving what is present in this season?

A Prayer

God,
Help me love without comparison.

Release me from the need to measure today
against yesterday.

Teach me to see dignity where I am,
and to love fully — right here.

Amen.

Permission for Today

You are allowed to love who she is now —
without guilt for missing who she was.

Reflections

Chapter 11
What I Wish Someone Had Told Me

I wish someone had told me that I would grieve long before I ever lost her.

That grief would not arrive all at once, but in small, aching moments — a forgotten name, a question asked twice, a story that no longer held its shape. I wish I had known that each of these would feel like a tiny goodbye, even though she was still sitting right in front of me.

No one warned me how often I would feel both love and sorrow at the same time.

I wish someone had told me that this was normal.

That I could be deeply grateful she was still here and still feel the sharp pain of what was slipping away. That these two truths could exist together without canceling each other out.

I spent a long time thinking I was doing something wrong because I was sad in the presence of someone I loved so much.

I wasn't doing anything wrong. I was grieving.

I wish someone had told me that I would need rest, not just physically, but emotionally. That caregiving would quietly stretch my heart in ways I couldn't have predicted. That it was not weakness to need a break, or to step outside for air, or to ask someone else to hold the moment for a while.

I thought love meant never stepping away.

I learned that love also means knowing when you need to be held.

I wish someone had told me that some days would feel manageable, and then — without warning — something would change. A new confusion. A new fear. A new loss. And it would feel like starting over again.

I wish I had known that this was not failure. It was simply the nature of this illness.

Dementia does not move in straight lines. It moves in waves.

You learn. You adjust. You find a rhythm.
And then the rhythm changes.

This is not because you are not doing enough. It is because this disease keeps changing the ground beneath your feet.

I wish someone had told me to enjoy what she could still do, even while I mourned what she could not.

To treasure the laughter, the moments of clarity, the small connections — not as denial, but as gratitude.

There would be days when her eyes met mine and I knew she felt safe. Days when she followed me from room to room, not because she was afraid, but because something in her remembered that I was home.

Those moments mattered.

They still do.

I wish someone had told me that I did not have to carry every part of this alone. That letting others help did not mean I loved her less. That even small acts — a sibling keeping her on the phone, a friend sitting with her, someone else answering a question — were not failures, but mercies.

Love was never meant to be a solo act.

I wish someone had told me that this kind of caregiving would change me.

That it would soften me in some places and harden me in others. That it would teach me patience I didn't know I had, and reveal limits I didn't know I needed to respect.

That it would show me what love looks like when there is nothing left to get in return.

And finally, I wish someone had told me that I would survive this.

That even on the days when it felt unbearable, I would still get up. Still love. Still show up. Still breathe.

That God would meet me not in my strength, but in my exhaustion.

That I would not be alone, even when it felt like I was.

If you are in this place now, consider this your gentle knowing:

You are not failing.
You are not weak.
You are not doing this wrong.

You are loving someone through one of the hardest seasons a heart can hold.

And that is more than enough.

Reflection

What are one or two things you wish someone had told you about this season?

Prayer

God, thank You for meeting me in this place.

When the weight feels too heavy, remind me that I am not alone and that You are holding both me and the one I love.

Give me the grace I need for today. Amen.

Permission for Today

You are allowed to rest.

You are allowed to ask for help.

You are allowed to love imperfectly and still be enough.

Reflections

Chapter 12

What This Season Has Taught Me About Love

This season has changed the way I understand love.

Before, I thought love was something you did —
something expressed through care, conversation,
shared plans, and mutual recognition.

I believed love was sustained by reciprocity.
By being known.
By being understood.

Dementia dismantled that framework.

It stripped love of familiarity and replaced it with
faithfulness.

I have learned that love is not proven by how much is
returned to you,
but by how steadily you remain when nothing comes
back.

Love, in this season, has taught me patience without affirmation.
Presence without reward.
Consistency without recognition.

It has taught me that love does not require clarity to be real.
It does not need memory to endure.
It does not disappear when understanding fades.

Love is quieter than I once believed.

It looks like repetition offered without irritation.
Reassurance given without explanation.
Care that continues even when it feels unseen.

This season has taught me that love is less about holding on
and more about showing up — again and again —
without demanding that things stay the same.

I have learned that love is not weakened by limits.

My limits did not diminish my devotion.
They refined it.

They taught me when to ask for help.
When to rest.
When to trust God with what I could not carry alone.

I also learned that I, too, needed gentleness. That love
was not just something I offered, but something I
needed to receive — especially in my own moments of
doubt and grief.

Love, I now see, is not sustained by control.
It is sustained by surrender.

This season reshaped not only how I love, but how I
understand womanhood, strength, and faith — lessons
that would later shape the way I walk alongside other
women.

This season also awakened a new urgency in me —
an awareness of how fragile time is, and how quickly
what we assume will remain can change.

I have learned not to postpone presence.
Not to delay gratitude.
Not to take for granted the ordinary moments that
quietly make up a life.

I am learning to live more fully in the now —
to appreciate each relationship while it is still available,
to say what needs to be said,
to love without assuming there will always be more
time.

There is grief in this season —
grief that does not resolve neatly,
grief that revisits without warning.

But love has met me there too.

It has taught me that grief is not the opposite of love.
It is one of its most honest expressions.

This season has taught me to love in the present tense.

Not the past I miss.
Not the future I fear.

But now.

To love what is still here.
To honor what has been.
To trust what I cannot see yet.

And perhaps most importantly, this season has taught
me
that love is not measured by outcomes.

It is measured by faithfulness.

By the quiet decision to stay.
To care.
To soften rather than harden.

To love — even when it looks different than you
imagined.

If you are walking through a season like this,
and wondering whether your love is enough, hear this:

It is.

It has always been.

And it will remain —
long after this season has passed.

Reflection

How has this season changed the way you see time,
love, and what truly matters?

A Prayer

God,
Thank You for the love You have taught me through this
season.

Teach me to live awake to each moment,
present to the people You have placed in my life.

Help me love without delay,
and trust You with what I cannot hold.

Amen.

Permission for Today

You are allowed to live fully now —
without waiting for a better season.

Reflections

Chapter 13
Small Rituals That Held Me

There were no grand solutions in this season.
No single practice that made things easier.

What sustained me were small, repeatable rituals —
moments of steadiness that did not fix anything, but
helped me remain.

These were not routines I perfected.
They were practices I returned to when I could.

Prayer and the study of Scripture became part of this
quiet holding — not as answers, but as anchors.

You may recognize some of these.
You may adapt them.
You may create your own.

They are offered here not as prescriptions, but as
possibilities.

Morning Orientation

Each morning, before the day began asking things of me,
I took a moment to orient myself.

Not to plan.
Not to prepare.

Simply to remember where I was.

A quiet breath.
A whispered prayer.
A reminder that I did not have to carry the entire day at
once.

This ritual did not make mornings easier.
It made them possible.

Returning to Scripture Without Urgency

There were days when I opened the Bible not looking
for clarity, instruction, or resolution.

I read slowly.
Sometimes only a verse.
Sometimes the same passage again.

I let the words be present without demanding that they explain my circumstances.

Scripture became a place to rest rather than a place to search for answers.

This gentle return steadied me.

Naming What Was Hard in Prayer

There were days when the most honest prayer I could offer was simply naming what felt heavy.

Not shaping it.
Not improving it.
Just saying it.

Naming gave shape to feelings that otherwise pressed inward.
It allowed weight to be held rather than absorbed.

Sometimes the prayer was a sentence.
Sometimes it was a word.
Sometimes it was silence.

All of it counted.

Permission to Pause

I learned to give myself permission to pause — without earning it.

Not after finishing everything.
Not after proving endurance.

Just because my body asked.

A pause might have been sitting in the car an extra minute.
Standing by a window.
Taking one breath longer than usual.

These pauses did not interrupt care.
They sustained it.

Returning to the Ordinary

Some days required anchoring in the ordinary.

Folding laundry.
Making tea or coffee.
Straightening a familiar space.

Ordinary tasks reminded me that not everything was unraveling.
They offered continuity when much felt uncertain.

This was not distraction.
It was grounding.

Protecting One Small Boundary

I could not protect everything.

But I could protect one thing.

A short walk.
A long run on some days.

A gym time.

A quiet hour.
A moment without conversation.

Keeping even a single boundary intact helped me remember that I existed beyond my role.

That reminder mattered more than I expected.

Ending the Day With Prayer

At the end of the day, I learned not to replay everything.

Instead, I returned to prayer — not to recount, but to release.

I asked one small question:
What did I do with care today?

The answer was rarely impressive.
It did not need to be.

Care, offered imperfectly, was enough to let the day rest.

These rituals did not remove grief.
They did not restore what was lost.

They simply gave me ways to stay.

If you find one small practice that steadies you,
let it be enough.

Care is sustained not by perfection,
but by what you return to.

Reflection

What small practice helped you stay

when you could not fix what was happening?

What did you return to

not for answers,

but for steadiness?

A Prayer

God,

Thank You for the ordinary ways You met me.

For small rituals that carried me

when I had little strength left.

Bless what was simple.

Bless what endured.

Amen.

Permission for Today

You are allowed to keep what sustained you.

You are allowed to release what no longer fits.

Faith does not have to be loud to be faithful.

Reflections

Chapter 14
What I Didn't Expect

What I Didn't Expect About Grief

I didn't expect grief to arrive while she was still here. I thought grief waited for endings — for funerals, for final breaths, for clear moments of loss. Instead, it came quietly, alongside ordinary days.

It showed up in small recognitions: a sentence that never finished, a memory that slipped away mid-thought, a look that searched for something familiar and didn't find it. Grief did not announce itself. It simply settled in.

What surprised me most was that grief did not replace love. It lived beside it. I could feel tenderness and sorrow at the same time, without either canceling the other. This kind of grief asked me not to let go, but to stay — to remain present inside something unresolved.

What I Didn't Expect About Time

I didn't expect time to feel so uneven. Some days stretched endlessly, filled with repetition and vigilance. Others passed quickly, leaving me startled by how much had changed without my noticing.

Time no longer moved forward in a straight line. It circled. It revisited old moments. It pulled memories into the present without warning. I learned that caring for someone with dementia alters your relationship with time itself.

What I didn't expect was how much I would learn to live in now — not because I wanted to, but because it became the only place that made sense.

What I Didn't Expect About My Own Strength

I didn't expect strength to feel this quiet. I had imagined strength as endurance — pushing through, holding together, remaining composed. Instead, it often looked like adaptation.

There were moments I felt unsure, moments I doubted myself, moments I wondered if I was doing enough.

Strength, I learned, was not certainty. It was showing up without guarantees.

I didn't expect how often strength would coexist with fatigue — how both could be true at once.

What I Didn't Expect About Communication

I didn't expect how much would still be communicated without words. When language became unreliable, I feared connection would disappear with it.

A look. A tone. A pause. Reassurance became more important than explanation. Presence replaced conversation.

What surprised me was how much meaning survived the loss of language — and how love learned to speak differently.

What I Didn't Expect About Fear

I didn't expect fear to become such a constant presence — not loud or dramatic, but steady and watchful.

Fear lived in vigilance, in scanning rooms, in anticipating needs before they were spoken. It existed because love was present — because there was something precious to protect.

I learned that courage did not mean eliminating fear. It meant continuing forward while carrying it.

What I Didn't Expect About Anger

I didn't expect anger to appear so quietly — or to feel so complicated. There was no clear target for it.

It surfaced in fatigue, repetition, and unfairness. Allowing myself to name anger honestly softened it.

Anger did not mean I loved less. It meant I was responding honestly to loss.

What I Didn't Expect About Faith

I didn't expect faith to feel thinner and quieter. I imagined reassurance; instead, I found presence.

Faith stayed with me inside uncertainty rather than resolving it.

It adapted, just like love did — becoming endurance rather than explanation.

What I Didn't Expect About Hope

I didn't expect hope to change shape. I once thought hope meant improvement or recovery.

Instead, hope became smaller and sturdier — rooted in moments rather than outcomes.

Hope learned to stay without promising anything beyond the present.

What I Didn't Expect About Love

I didn't expect love to remain so intact. I thought it depended on recognition and familiarity.

Instead, love adapted. It endured. It stayed present even as roles shifted.

Love did not need to be fixed or explained. It simply remained.

Reflection

What changed in you

that you did not plan for?

What did this season teach you

without asking your permission?

A Prayer

God,

Thank You for meeting me

in what I did not expect.

Help me carry forward what is true

and lay down what is heavy.

Amen.

Permission for Today

You are allowed to move forward

without full understanding.

You are allowed to be changed

and still be whole.

Reflections

Letters for the Caregiver

To the one who feels alone

There is a loneliness that comes from carrying responsibility rather than lacking company. You may be surrounded by people who care, and still feel as though no one quite stands where you are standing. This kind of loneliness is not a failure of support — it is the result of loving someone in a way that cannot be fully shared.

You have become the keeper of details others do not see. The one who notices the shifts, anticipates the needs, holds the worry quietly so it does not spread. That role can make the world feel smaller, even when your heart feels fuller.

If you have wondered why this feels isolating despite love around you, let yourself rest in this truth: some paths are narrow because they are precise, not because you are meant to walk them unsupported. You are not unseen — you are simply doing something few are asked to do.

To the one who is strong for everyone else

There is a kind of strength that is rarely acknowledged — the kind that steadies others while quietly setting itself aside. You may be the one people look to, assume can manage, trust to carry more without asking how heavy it feels.

Strength, in this season, has likely meant composure. Reliability. Making room for other people's emotions while holding your own privately. You have learned how to be capable even when you are unsure, steady even when you are tired.

If strength has begun to feel like invisibility, let this be said: being strong for others does not obligate you to disappear. You are allowed to need care, softness, and rest — even if you are the one who usually provides it.

To the one who feels anger and love at the same time

You may have been surprised by the coexistence of these emotions. Love that remains steady. Anger that arrives without invitation. Both true. Both real.

Anger does not mean your love has weakened. Often, it means love has encountered limits — of fairness, of endurance, of control. It arises not because you care less, but because you care deeply inside a situation that offers no easy resolution.

You do not need to choose between these emotions. They can occupy the same space without canceling one another. Let anger inform you, not define you. Let love remain the deeper current.

To the one whose faith feels thin

There may be days when faith feels less like confidence and more like endurance. Less like answers and more like showing up again without clarity. If belief has become quieter, more tentative, you are not failing it.

Faith does not always look like certainty. Sometimes it looks like staying present in what you cannot explain. Like continuing to care even when prayers feel unfinished. Like trusting that presence still matters when resolution does not arrive.

If your faith feels thinner, it may be because it is being stretched — not lost. You are allowed to rest inside questions. Faith does not leave when certainty does.

To the one who fears what comes next

Fear may surface when you think ahead — not dramatically, but persistently. Questions about progression, capacity, endurance. About how much more change you can absorb.

You are not required to hold the entire future at once. Fear often grows when it is asked to imagine everything ahead of time. You may find steadiness not by looking forward, but by returning to what is asked of you today.

The fact that you fear what comes next does not mean you are unprepared. It means you understand the weight of what you are carrying. Courage, here, is staying present without demanding certainty.

To the one who is learning to receive help

Receiving help can feel unfamiliar — even uncomfortable — especially if you are used to being the one others rely on. You may have learned independence early, competence quickly, self-sufficiency as a form of safety.

Accepting help does not mean you have reached a breaking point. It means you recognize that care was never meant to be solitary. Support does not replace your love; it makes space for it to continue.

Learning to receive is its own form of strength. It asks for humility, trust, and honesty about limits. These are not weaknesses. They are what allow care to endure.

To the one who is still becoming herself

This season may have reshaped you quietly. Altered how you see responsibility, patience, love, and yourself. You may notice parts of who you were receding, and parts of someone new emerging.

Be gentle with this becoming. You are not losing yourself — you are being formed by circumstances that require depth, attentiveness, and restraint. These qualities do not diminish you. They refine you.

You are allowed to grow without fully understanding who you are becoming. Identity is not fixed in moments of care; it is revealed slowly. And you are allowed to take your time.

To the one who is tired

This tiredness is not only physical. It comes from staying alert when others sleep, from listening closely even when words no longer arrive cleanly, from being the steady one when steadiness is required again and again.

You may have reached a point where rest feels incomplete — where sleep helps the body but not the weight you carry during the day. If so, allow yourself to name this as fatigue that deserves compassion, not correction.

You are not weak because you are tired. You are tired because you have been faithful in ways that ask much of a person. There is dignity in acknowledging that weariness rather than pushing past it. Let tiredness be a signal to soften, not to disappear.

To the one learning to grieve slowly

This grief does not announce itself with finality. It arrives in fragments — a change in tone, a missing word, a moment that does not return. It asks you to grieve not once, but repeatedly, without the closure most losses provide.

If you find yourself unsure whether what you feel "counts" as grief, know this: grief does not require an ending to be real. It only requires love and change.

You are learning a kind of mourning that moves alongside daily life, one that allows joy to coexist without resolution. This is not confusion. It is adaptation. And it is one of the hardest forms of grief to carry with grace.

To the one holding vigil

There are hours when nothing is asked of you except presence — and yet presence costs everything. Staying when there is no progress, no improvement, no clarity can feel invisible in a world that measures effort by outcomes.

But staying is not passive. It is a quiet offering. It is attention given without expectation. It is love that does not require return.

If you have wondered whether these moments matter, let this be said clearly: vigil is one of the most faithful postures of love. Even when nothing changes, you do.

To the one learning to live with uncertainty

Uncertainty has become a constant companion. Plans feel tentative, expectations easily disrupted, the future less cooperative than it once was. You may find yourself holding life more loosely, not because you want to, but because you have learned you must.

Living this way requires courage that is rarely acknowledged. It asks you to release certainty without surrendering care. To remain engaged without guarantees.

If you feel unsettled by how much remains unknown, remember this: steadiness is not the absence of uncertainty. It is the decision to remain present within it. And you are already doing that.

To the one holding joy and sorrow at once

You may have wondered if it is possible to laugh and grieve in the same day.
It is. You are living proof.

Joy does not betray grief.
Grief does not cancel joy.
They are not opposites — they are companions now.

If moments of lightness catch you by surprise, you do not need to apologize for them.
They are not signs of forgetting.
They are signs that love is still alive, learning how to breathe in a changed world.

To the one who misses being known

There was a time when you were understood without explanation.
When shared history filled in the gaps.
When being seen did not require translation.

It is okay to miss that ease.
Missing does not mean you are ungrateful for what remains.

It means you remember who you were together.
And remembering, too, is a form of love.

To the version of you who comes later

There may come a day when this season feels distant —
not erased, but quieter.
When the sharpness has softened, and memory no
longer presses as heavily on your chest.

If that day comes, I hope you remember this version of
yourself with kindness.

Remember that you did not know everything, but you
showed up anyway.
That you learned as you went.
That you loved without guarantees.

There were moments you felt unsure, moments you
wished you could do better, moments you wondered if
you were enough.
I hope you know now that you were.

If you ever feel tempted to judge the choices you made
here, pause.

You made them with the information, strength, and love
you had at the time.
That was enough.

Carry forward what this season taught you —
the patience,
the attentiveness,
the ability to sit with what cannot be fixed.

And if one day life feels lighter, do not feel guilty for that
either.
Joy does not betray what came before.
It honors it.

Wherever you are when you read this, may you
remember:
you loved deeply,
you stayed honest,
and you learned how to remain.

That part of you does not fade.

For the Days When...

For the days when you feel unseen

There are kinds of work that leave no visible trace.
No milestones.
No applause.

And yet, they shape lives quietly.

If today feels unnoticed, remember:
what is unseen is not unimportant.
Love does not require witnesses to be real.

For the days when you miss who they used to be

Missing does not mean you are rejecting who she is
now.
It means you are holding more than one truth at once.

You can love who stands before you
and grieve who once stood beside you.

Both belong.

For the days when patience runs thin

Patience is not an endless resource.
It stretches.
It frays.
It asks to be renewed.

If today you feel short-tempered or weary,
let that be information, not accusation.

Rest is not failure.
It is maintenance.

For the days when guilt speaks loudly

Guilt often appears when love has no clear outlet.
When effort feels insufficient.
When care has limits.

Listen gently.
Then remind yourself:
you are allowed to be finite.

Love does not demand depletion.

For the days when words fail you

There may be moments when language disappears.
When nothing you say feels right or useful.

Presence is still communication.
So is touch.
So is simply staying.

Silence, too, can be a form of care.

For the days when you long for relief

Wanting this season to be easier does not make you
disloyal.
It makes you human.

Relief is not the same as escape.
It is the body asking for mercy.

Listen without shame.

For the days when joy surprises you

Joy may arrive unexpectedly —
in laughter, memory, or a quiet moment of peace.

You do not need to push it away.
Joy does not erase grief.

It rests alongside it.

*For the days when you wonder who you are
becoming*

Caregiving reshapes identity.
Not abruptly, but steadily.

If you feel changed,
it is because you are.

Change does not mean loss.
It often means depth.

For the days when others misunderstand

There may be moments when well-meaning people offer explanations instead of presence. When advice comes easily, but understanding does not. When your reality is simplified in ways that leave you feeling unseen.

You are not obligated to translate this season into something comfortable for others. Some experiences resist explanation — not because you lack words, but because the weight cannot be shared evenly.

Misunderstanding does not invalidate your experience. It simply reminds you that not everyone is meant to stand where you are standing.

For the days when you feel resentful

Resentment may surface quietly, without warning. Toward circumstances. Toward the constancy of responsibility. Toward the way life has narrowed around care.

If resentment appears, let it be named without judgment. It is often a sign of exhaustion, not a lack of love. Love can endure while still asking for relief.

Feeling resentful does not mean you are ungrateful. It means you are human inside a demanding season.

For the days when you feel relief — and guilt

There may be moments when things are calm. When responsibility lightens briefly. When you feel relief — and immediately question it.

Relief does not betray devotion. It does not cancel care. It simply means you are responding to the easing of pressure.

You are not required to suffer continuously in order to prove love. Peace, when it comes, is allowed to stay.

For the days when you want to be alone

Wanting solitude does not mean you are withdrawing from love. It often means you are listening to your own limits.

Caregiving requires constant attentiveness. Wanting space may be the body's way of asking for quiet — not absence, but restoration.

Taking time alone does not mean you are abandoning anyone. It means you are preserving yourself.

For the days when you don't recognize yourself

There may be moments when you feel unfamiliar to yourself. When reactions surprise you. When patience, certainty, or ease feel harder to access.

This does not mean you are becoming someone you don't want to be. It means you are being shaped by responsibility, grief, and love held over time.

Change does not always announce itself gently. But it often carries depth you have not yet learned to see.

For the days when love feels quiet

Love may no longer look like conversation, recognition, or shared memory. It may arrive instead as presence. As repetition. As staying.

If love feels quieter now, it is not because it has diminished. It has simply changed form.

Quiet love is still love. Often, it is the kind that endures the longest.

For the days when the future feels too far away

You are not required to understand what comes next. Only what is asked of you today.

This moment is enough.
So are you.

How to Show Up for a Caregiver

Most people want to help.
Many simply do not know how.

This section is not written to instruct perfectly, but to orient gently.
It is for friends, family members, colleagues, and communities who want to show up — and for caregivers who may want language to share without having to explain themselves.

What Caregivers Often Carry Silently

Caregiving is not only about tasks.
It is about anticipation, vigilance, and emotional labor
that rarely announces itself.

Caregivers often carry:
• Decisions that feel heavy and unfinished
• Responsibility that does not pause
• Grief that arrives without ceremony
• Love that adapts daily

Much of this is invisible. Not because it is insignificant,
but because it has become constant.

What Helps More Than You Might Realize

Help does not need to be dramatic to be meaningful.
It needs to be specific, reliable, and kind.

What helps:
• Offering concrete support rather than general
availability
• Checking in without requiring updates
• Remembering important dates, routines, or

preferences
- Showing up more than once

Consistency builds trust. Presence builds relief.

What Often Hurts (Even When It's Well-Intended)

Many well-meaning responses unintentionally add weight.

These include:
- Minimizing loss because the person is still alive
- Offering comparisons or silver linings
- Giving advice instead of presence
- Praising strength without noticing cost

Caregivers rarely need forced optimism that minimizes their reality.
They need to be believed — and then supported.

What to Say When You Don't Know What to Say

You do not need the right words.
You need honest ones.

Helpful phrases include:
- "This looks heavy. I'm here."
- "You don't have to explain."
- "Would it help if I handled something this week?"
- "I can stay while you take a break."

Simple language, offered sincerely, often lands best.

How to Offer Help That Lasts

Initial support often fades as time passes.
Care, however, does not.

Sustainable support looks like:
- Returning after the crisis moment
- Setting reminders to check in
- Taking on recurring tasks
- Being comfortable with repetition

Longevity matters more than intensity.

If You Are Not Sure What Is Needed

When in doubt, do something small.
Then come back.
Then come back again.

Care is built through repetition.
Not grand gestures.

A Note for Caregivers Reading This

You are allowed to share this section.
You are allowed to ask for what you need.
You are allowed to let others learn.

Care was never meant to be carried alone.
Receiving support does not diminish your love.
It helps it endure.

Showing up does not require expertise.
It requires attention.

When presence is offered without pressure or explanation,
caregivers are reminded that they are not invisible —
and not alone.

A Resource Map

Ways to find support without having to know everything at once.

You do not need all of these resources.

You do not need them at the same time.

You may not need some at all.

This map is not a checklist.

It is simply a reminder that support exists — and that reaching for it can happen slowly.

When You Need Immediate Support

If you are feeling overwhelmed, unsafe, or unable to cope, consider reaching out to:

• A trusted family member or friend

• Your primary care provider

• A mental health professional

• Local emergency or crisis services if safety is a concern

Asking for immediate help is not a failure.

It is a form of care.

When medical questions or care logistics feel heavy, support may include:
• Primary care physicians or specialists involved in dementia care
• Geriatric care managers
• Social workers connected to clinics or hospitals
• Memory care clinics or neurology practices

These professionals can help with:
• Understanding progression
• Navigating care decisions
• Connecting you to local resources

You are allowed to ask the same question more than once.

Community & Caregiver Support

Many caregivers find steadiness in spaces where explanation is unnecessary:
• Local caregiver support groups
• Faith-based or community organizations

- Dementia-focused nonprofits
- Online caregiver communities

Support groups are not for everyone.
But for some, being understood without speaking is relief.

Respite & Practical Help

Care is sustained when rest is possible.

Support may include:
- In-home respite services
- Adult day programs
- Rotational family support
- Paid caregiving assistance, when accessible

Taking breaks does not diminish devotion.
It protects it.

Emotional & Mental Health Support

Caregiving changes the emotional landscape.

You may benefit from:
- Therapy or counseling
- Spiritual direction or pastoral care
- Journaling or reflective practices
- Supportive friendships that do not require updates

You are allowed to tend to your inner life while caring for another.

Legal & Planning Support

Some support is quiet but stabilizing:
- Advance care planning
- Power of attorney guidance
- Financial or estate planning
- Care planning conversations

You do not need to do all of this at once.
Planning can happen in pieces.

If You Don't Know Where to Start

Begin with one question:
"What feels heaviest right now?"

Then look for support that meets that need — not every possible one.

Care does not require mastery.
It requires honesty.

A Gentle Reminder

Support is not something you earn after exhaustion. It is something you are allowed to receive along the way.

You were never meant to do this alone.

A Month of Gentle Prompts

These prompts are invitations, not assignments.

You may use them daily, weekly, or only when
something stirs.
You may write a page, a sentence, or nothing at all.

There is no right pace.
There is only honesty.

What feels heaviest today?

What did I carry silently?

What did love look like today?

What am I tired of explaining?

What deserves gentleness right now?

What can wait and what cannot?

Where did I feel stretched thin?

What helped more than I expected?

What am I missing?

What am I allowed to miss?

Where do I need rest, not answers?

What would "enough" mean today?

What did I survive this week?

What feels unresolved — and may remain so?

What am I learning about myself?

Where do grief and gratitude overlap?

What emotion surprised me today?

What did I let go of, even briefly?

What am I afraid to name?

What steadied me?

What do I need support with right now?

What can I stop doing alone?

What has changed me in quiet ways?

What remains meaningful?

What kind of care do I need?

What would help me breathe easier?

What can I offer myself?

What does love look like now?

What do I want to remember?

What Remains — A Closing Benediction

You did not imagine this season.

It was as heavy as it felt.

You did not fail it.

You stayed.

You did not love incorrectly.

You loved in changing conditions.

You were asked to adapt without instruction,

to grieve without an ending,

to remain present without reassurance.

And you did.

You learned how to give without being certain.

You learned how to stay when things did not resolve.

You learned how to let love change shape without letting it disappear.

What you offered mattered.

Even when it went unseen.

Even when it felt incomplete.

Memory is not the measure of meaning.

Recognition is not the measure of love.

Ease is not the measure of faithfulness.

You were faithful in ways that will never be tallied.

If you are tired, let that be honest.

If you are relieved, let that be allowed.

If you are changed, let that be honored.

This season did not take everything from you.

It gave you depth.

It gave you attentiveness.

It gave you a way of loving that does not depend on return.

As you move forward—

into whatever comes next—

may you carry less explanation

and more gentleness.

Toward yourself.

Toward others.

Toward the life still unfolding.

And if there is one truth to hold onto, let it be this:

Even as memory fades,

even as roles shift,

even as language falls short—

the love that remains is real, enduring, and still yours.

A Note on Giving Back

A portion of the proceeds from this book is donated to organizations that support people living with dementia and the caregivers who walk beside them.

This book was written as an offering — a way of naming a kind of love that is often unseen.

Allowing it to also support those doing this work in the world felt like a natural extension of that same care.

Your reading makes that possible. In quiet ways, it allows this story — and the love behind it — to reach beyond these pages.

Whether or not you ever think about this again, please know that your reading is already part of something good.

About the Author

Dr. Toyin Olubiyi is a physician, entrepreneur, wife, mother, and daughter.

She wrote this book while caring for her mother through dementia — a season that reshaped how she understands love, faith, and presence. Though trained in medicine, this book was written not from clinical expertise, but from lived experience, reflection, and prayer.

Her writing is rooted in faith, presence, and the belief that growth does not always look like striving — sometimes it looks like staying, surrendering, and loving faithfully. She also leads community groups at her local church, walking alongside others through changing seasons.

She lives with her husband and children, carrying this season alongside family, community, and grace.